—Weird and Wacky Science—

MEAT-EATING PLANTS

Nathan Aaseng

ENSLOW PUBLISHERS, INC.

44 Fadem Road
Box 699
Springfield, N.J. 07081
U.S.A.

P.O. Box 38
Aldershot
Hants GU12 6BP
U.K.

Library of Congress Cataloging-in-Publication Data

Aaseng, Nathan.
    Meat-eating plants / by Nathan Aaseng.
        p. cm. — (Weird and wacky science)
    Includes bibliographical references (p.) and index.
    ISBN 0-89490-617-8
    1. Carnivorous plants—Juvenile literature. [1. Carnivorous plants.]
    I. Title. II. Series.
    QK917.A2 1996
    582'.121—dc20   95-3827
                                                                          CIP
                                                                           AC

Printed in the United States of America

10 9 8 7 6 5 4 3 2

Illustration Credits: Timothy Smalley, pp. 20, 32; State of Minnesota, pp. 12, 14, 34, 40; Visuals
Unlimited: © Tom Adams, p. 33; © Cabisco, pp. 4, 10, 28; John D. Cunningham, p. 19; ©Max &
Bea Hunn, p. 36; © Howard A. Miller, Sr., p. 22; ©D. Newman, p. 7; © Dick Poe, p. 17; © Kjell B.
Sandved, p. 27; © Milton H. Tierney, Jr., p. 39; ©Peter K. Ziminksi, p. 25.

Cover Illustration: © Breck P. Kent/Animals, Animals.

Contents

1. Green Monsters and Killer Fungi

5

2. Flypaper Traps

13

3. Pitfall Traps

21

4. Trigger Traps

29

5. Endless Quest for Survival

35

Notes by Chapter

43

Glossary

44

Classification

45

Further Reading

46

Index

47

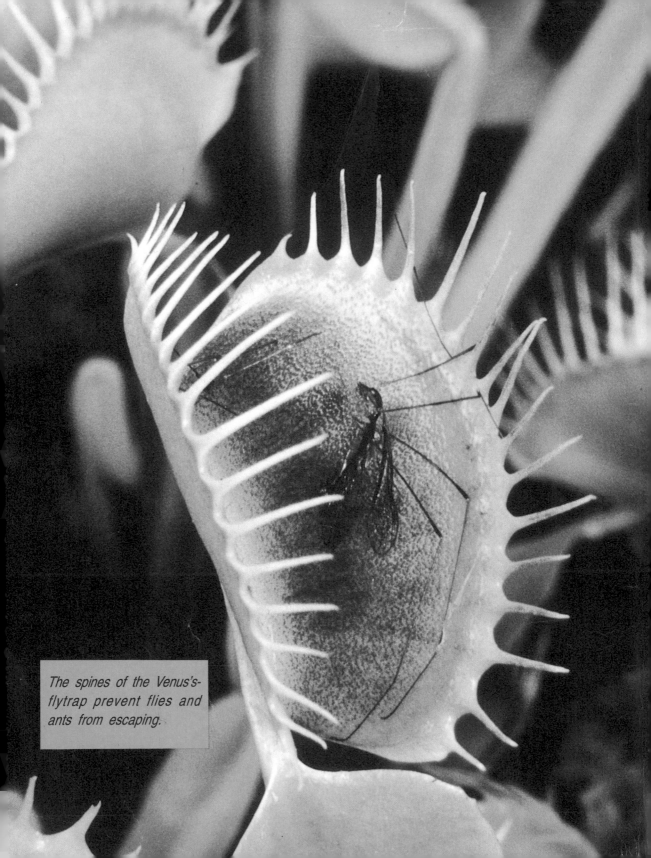

The spines of the Venus's-flytrap prevent flies and ants from escaping.

1

GREEN MONSTERS AND KILLER FUNGI

About a hundred years ago, a doctor reported a hideous event that he had seen in the island of Madagascar. He described a tribe sacrificing a girl to a flesh-eating tree. The deadly plant stood ten feet (three meters) high. Its twelve-foot-long leaves bristled with sharp spikes. According to the doctor, the plant snared the girl in its long, snakelike tendrils. Then the murderous leaves closed in on her and finished her off.[1]

Other reports of huge, deadly plants have surfaced over the years. A plant in Brazil was said to lure monkeys with bright flowers and sweet aromas. Then it crushed and consumed them. Sailors in the South Pacific were warned to avoid an island where the Death Flower grew. This plant was said to form a gorgeous cave so large that people could walk into it. If they did so, the overpowering aroma would put them to sleep. The plant would then devour its unconscious victim.[2]

The idea of such deadly plants continues to fascinate us. Science fiction writers often tell tales of killer tomatoes and other lethal plants that stalk humans and other large animals. One of the most popular of these tales has been *The Little Shop of Horrors*, which has been made into both a Broadway musical and a movie. In this story, a rare and valuable plant requires human blood in order to survive. As it grows ever larger, these demands grow ever more gruesome.

Any educated person now recognizes such reports as fantasies produced by overactive imaginations. While our planet holds a wondrous variety of plants, it does not contain any that feast on humans or even on monkeys.

The very notion of plants eating animals is bizarre; it seems backward. Plants are at the bottom of the food chain. They provide meals for animals. We think of meat eaters as deadly creatures equipped with sharp teeth, claws, brute strength, and speed. Plants do not fit that description. Many plants cannot even defend themselves from baby rabbits, fat caterpillars, or tiny aphids. They do not have mouths or stomachs for digesting meals. How could they possibly eat animals?

Searching for Killer Plants

The idea of plants eating animals seemed so absurd that, for hundreds of years, plant experts discounted such talk. True, plants had developed some weapons that could hurt animals, such as the sharp thorns of the rose and the blackberry. Plants had poisons in their leaves and stems that could kill animals. Certain plants with sticky leaves

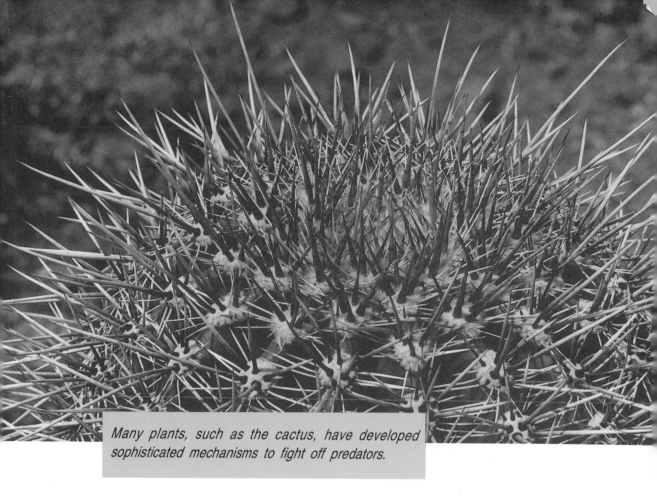

Many plants, such as the cactus, have developed sophisticated mechanisms to fight off predators.

were so adept at trapping small insects that people hung them in their houses as pest control. These were all believed to be the ways plants protected themselves from animals. After all, how could plants eat animals?

In the eighteenth century, English settlers in America found a plant they called a Venus's-flytrap. They watched this plant snap shut and squeeze insects. Could this plant be trapping and eating these insects? No, said the experts. The trap was just another ingenious way for the plant to protect itself against pests.[3]

For many years people had noticed pools of water inside the pitcher plants that grew in North America and in the Pacific tropics. Some discovered dead insects floating in that liquid. Near the end of the eighteenth century, American botanist (a person who studies plants) William Bartram grew curious about some features of these plants. He observed that certain downward-pointing hairs in the plant seemed to invite insects to the water, where they died. Again, that could be yet another example of a plant defending itself by killing off possible enemies.

In 1857, a researcher named Cohn examined one of the tiny sacs on an aquatic plant called a bladderwort. Most people who knew of these sacs thought that they served as buoys to keep the plant afloat, but when the researcher opened one up, he discovered a tiny dead fish. About twenty years later, researcher Mary Treat found that the sac was a trap that could engulf tiny water creatures in the blink of an eye.

By this time, many experts suspected that these plants were actually doing the unexpected—devouring small animals. By the late nineteenth century, the famous biologist Charles Darwin proved once and for all that plants did eat animals. He found that these plants produced enzymes, much like the digestive enzymes found in animals. Furthermore, his careful measurements showed that the plants actually were absorbing nutrients from the dead creatures. Darwin's experiments also showed that carnivorous— or meat-eating—plants that were fed an occasional meaty meal were more healthy than those that were given no meat.

Carnivorous Plant Family

Since Darwin's time, botanists have identified more than six hundred species of carnivorous plants. Insect-eating plants live in all parts of the world, in many types of climates from the arctic to the tropics.

Most live in places with wet, spongy soil, called bogs. The wetlands and bogs along the Gulf coast of the United States are teeming with carnivorous plants. As many as thirteen species have been found crowded together within a few acres.

Most of these plants are fairly small. There are no killer trees or human-eating plants for us to worry about, but there are plants capable of devouring animals as large as rats, mice, lemurs, frogs, snakes, and small birds. Others dine on scorpions, spiders, grasshoppers, wasps, flies, ants, slugs, snails, baby fish, and tadpoles.

Even the smaller plant carnivores are no less fascinating for their size. Some of the smaller animals in our world must indeed tread carefully around killer plants.

Beware the killer grasses! *Molinia caerulea*, for example, is a grass that catches and eats insects for a brief time in its life. The grass has small traps on it that spring shut on small prey.

Beware the killer fungi! One fungus, called *Arthrobotrys obligiospora*, contains looped structures. The loop draws tight as tiny creatures, such as eelworms, crawl through it. The fungus then digests its victim. Another fungus, *Zoophagus insidians*, sets a trap for minute animals called *rotatoria*. It sends out short branches for the rotatoria to feed on. As the rotatorium takes a bite, the tip of the branch swells, and the feeder is trapped.

Some small animals must even beware of killer seeds! Seeds of a plant known as *Capsella bursa-pastoris* use a pleasant chemical aroma to attract mosquito larvae. When the larvae arrive, the seeds release a poison that kills them. The seeds then release an enzyme to digest the prey so that it can be absorbed.

Killer fungi can trap and digest tiny creatures.

Most carnivorous plants appear quite harmless. They do not have the intimidating presence of a tiger or a grizzly bear. They look innocent, peaceful, even inviting. The carnivorous plants are among the most beautiful in nature, with delicate flowers of yellow, purple, and white. Their leaves may be etched with intricate designs of green, purple, red, and pink.

Hidden within this attractive beauty are deadly traps that make these plants as effective at capturing prey as the most feared animals. Some plants kill and consume thousands of mosquito larvae in their lifetime. Some have developed such foolproof trapping methods that they can collect hundreds of prey in a single day.

A British scientist once wandered across a killing field that clearly showed both the carnivorous plants' incredible beauty and their deadly menace to small creatures. A dense carpet of low-growing sundew plants spread for nearly two acres in a remote, spongy bog. Droplets of clear liquid like diamonds sparkled on each plant.

A huge cloud of migrating butterflies swarmed onto the meadow for a rest before they continued their journey. They never left. The butterflies stuck to the little jeweled droplets and could not escape. As many as seven butterflies writhed in their death throes on a single plant. The scientist estimated that this sundew stand killed 6 million butterflies in a single afternoon![4]

The leaves of this butterwort (Pinguicula vulgaria) are littered with prey.

2

FLYPAPER TRAPS

The simplest way that plants snare victims is the flypaper technique. This method is used by the *Pinguicula*, or butterworts, plants that you would hardly expect to be carnivorous. You could study the plants' structure carefully and not guess that they feed on tiny animals.

Butterworts

Butterworts thrive in most parts of the world north of the Equator. They are the kind of plant that easily blends into the background. Their yellow-green leaves lie flat to the ground in a crowded circle pattern called a rosette. These leaves appear to be greasy rather than sticky. In fact, their name comes from the buttery feel of the

Sundew (Drosera rotundifolia) *tentacles await a meal.*

leaves. Only the tiniest, lightest insects need fear getting trapped in this coating.

A tiny gnat flying through the air detects a sweet aroma. It locates the source of this attractive smell: a small butterwort. The gnat lands on one of the leaves. Too late, the insect discovers that the aroma was a lure. Its legs are now stuck in the greasy substance. The gnat struggles to get free. As it does, the plant produces more of the greasy substance. Before long the thrashing gnat is so coated with the substance that it suffocates and dies.

The butterwort then releases enzymes to digest the nutrients in the insect. The leaf curls slightly to form a shallow saucer, which keeps the enzymes from spilling out. This is especially important when rain washes over the plant. The butterwort also bathes the dead gnat in an antibiotic. This kills bacteria feeding on the prey that might spread and cause harm to the plant.

Butterworts are not fussy eaters. Few other carnivorous plants will consume plants as well as animals. The plant leaves will curl up and digest anything, including seeds and small bits of plant material, that contains nitrogen, which is present in all living things.

Sundews

The *Drosera*, or sundews, are somewhat more lively flypaper killers. Rather than waiting for the prey to kill itself, the sundews work to make the job go faster.

More than a hundred species of sundews grow throughout the world, although most species occur in Australia.[1] They live in many types of climates. Like the butterworts, sundews often hide beneath other plants, their leaves clustered low to the ground.

Some grow less than an inch high, while other varieties can grow more than two feet (sixty centimeters) tall.[2]

Sundews are strikingly beautiful, especially when their crystal-clear beads of nectar, which look like morning dew, glisten in the sun. These beads rest on top of tentacles, which are thin, reddish, hairlike stalks that rise up from the sundew's flat leaves.

A butterfly fluttering over a field detects the sweet nectar of a sundew and stops to take a sample. As soon as it lands, it finds that the nectar is combined with an extremely sticky substance called mucilage. The butterfly's legs get caught. It tries to pull away from the mucilage.

This struggle signals the sundew to kill the butterfly. The plant has a unique way of sorting out a meal from a piece of dust, or dirt, or a raindrop. Although these things may be heavier than the insects that alight on it, the plant will not waste time and energy on them. Only when it feels movement will it prepare for the kill.

The sundew's glands send out more mucilage. As the butterfly tries to pull away, mucilage gloms on to its wing. Meanwhile, tentacles begin to arch toward the insect. The plant has no central nervous system to coordinate movement the way animals can, yet somehow each tentacle on the leaf gets the message to bend in the right direction toward the prey.

The butterfly becomes desperate. The harder it fights, the faster the tentacles move, and the more mucilage pours out of the leaf. Eventually, the sticky tentacles reach the butterfly and press it down into the mucilage. The butterfly drowns in the sticky fluid. The sundew then releases acids and enzymes to digest the victim.

A dragonfly is stuck on a deadly sundew.

Some sundews have tentacles that can curl over the prey within a minute. Others do not reach the insect for many hours. These tentacles do not aid in the kill, but they do aid digestion by holding the prey in the fluid. Some have leaves that fold around the prey for the same purpose. A few sundews have such powerful digestive systems that they can absorb a prey's nutrients in a matter of hours.[3]

When the sundew is finished with the prey, the tentacles relax their grip, and the undigested shell of the insect falls away. It may take a week or two before the tentacles straighten up to their original position. Each leaf can capture three or four meals before it loses its ability to fold in on prey. It then dies and is replaced by a new leaf.

Sundews can be deadly killers of insects. Botanists commonly find the shells of six or more insects on a single leaf. One researcher reported finding a sundew that had more than a hundred insects in its sticky grip.[4]

Byblis

The *Byblis* are a less common form of flypaper killer. These beautiful purple-flowered plants grow in Australia. One species reaches a height of more than two feet (sixty centimeters) and can intertwine with other *Byblis* plants to form a woody hedge.[5] It has been reported that sometimes *Byblis* hedges capture and digest small lizards and frogs that try to eat the plants' insect prey.

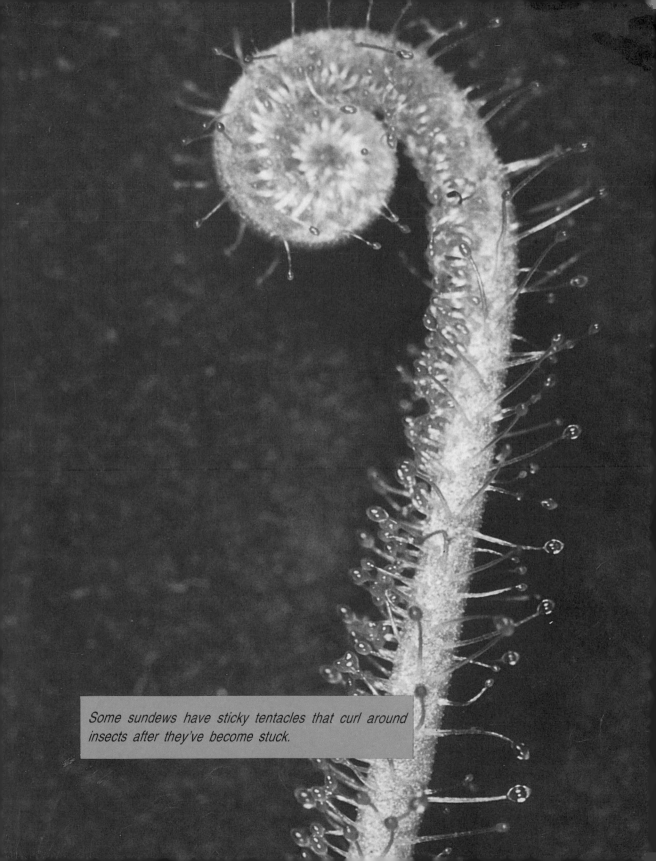

Some sundews have sticky tentacles that curl around insects after they've become stuck.

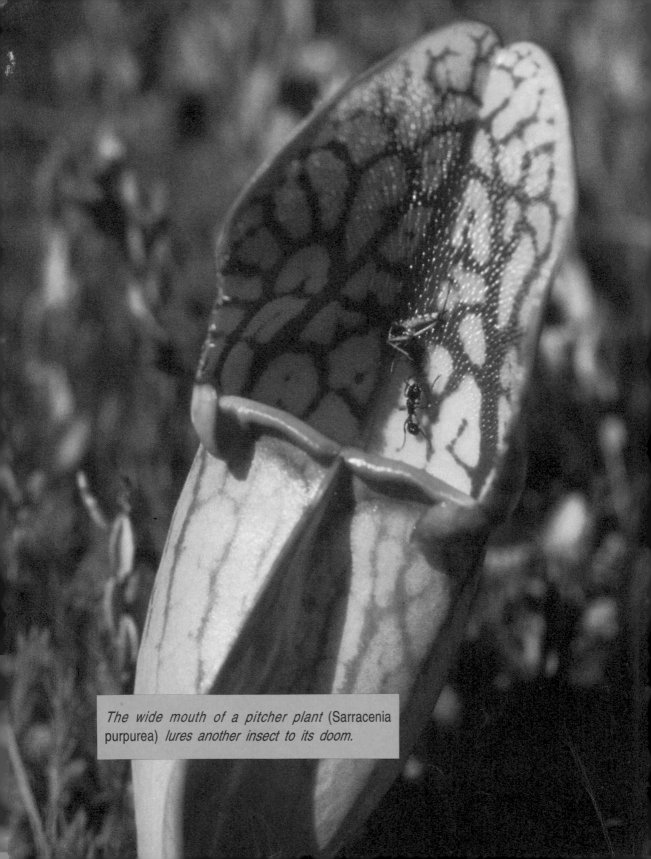

The wide mouth of a pitcher plant (Sarracenia purpurea) lures another insect to its doom.

3

PITFALL TRAPS

While slogging through a bog along Alabama's Gulf Coast or in Minnesota's northern wetlands, you might come across a field carpeted with *Sarracenia*, or pitcher plants. Row after row of these beautiful plants with their green and purple graceful, trumpet-shaped leaves and dangling yellow flowers spread before you.

What looks like a peaceful display of nature's delicate beauty is misleading. Once you know the fiendishly clever lengths these plants go to snare their victims, you can almost begin to hear that eerie music they play in scary scenes of movies.

Pitcher plants have developed a more complex method of capturing meals than that of the flypaper trappers. Like the flypapers, they do not actively subdue their prey, but they present such a well-designed pitfall trap that the victim can't resist walking straight to its death.

Pitcher plants are common in North America, especially in low-lying, damp, sandy areas. The pitchers are long leaves that rise from an underground stem called a rhizome. The form a hollow, vaselike tube that is usually narrow at the bottom and wider near the top—the open end of the pitcher. Part of the leaf forms a hood over the opening.

A pitcher plant is loaded with lures. Its bright, graceful leaves and sweet aroma entice insects. The hood provides shelter for

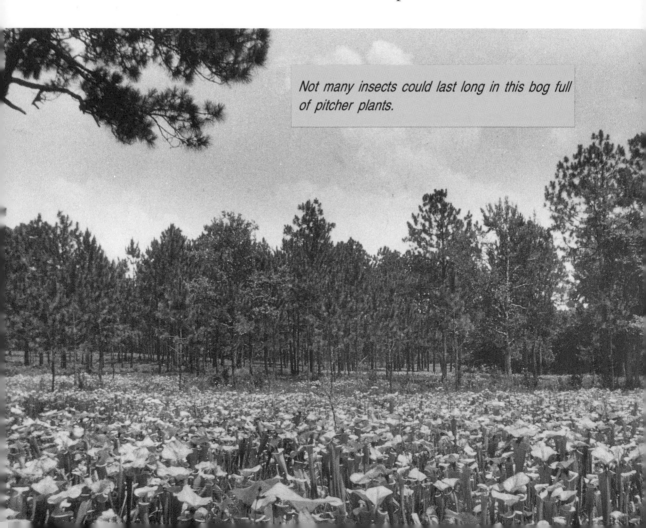

Not many insects could last long in this bog full of pitcher plants.

insects and other small creatures who want to escape the rain. The undersurface of the hood contains nectar glands that produce a sugary treat that insects enjoy. Some pitcher plants lay a trail of nectar that starts at ground level and leads up to the mouth of the pitcher.

The Trap

Once the prey lands on the hood, the pitcher plant lures it further into the pitcher. The plant provides an even greater store of sweet nectar down at the mouth. The hood and parts of the neck of the pitcher often lack color. These areas allow light to shine down into the pitcher, so that insects are not afraid to go into it. The insect may even sense the pool of liquid at the bottom of the pitcher and believe it is more nectar.

As the insect moves toward the mouth, it may slip on the smooth surface into a region lined with stiff hairs. These hairs provide poor footing.

At this point, the insect may sense something is not quite right about this easy meal. It may stop eating for brief periods, perhaps trying to sense where the danger is coming from. It may sense that the hairs mean trouble. Some insects try to reach over the hairs to get at the rich pool of nectar on the other side, but the nectar is just out of reach, so that the insect will have to stretch far, and possibly fall down into the pitcher.

After a time, a flying insect may try to get out while the getting is good, but the colorless hood lets in so much light that it appears to be an opening to the outside. The insect flies toward it, smashes into the hood, and falls down into the pitcher. Some kinds of pitchers are spotted with uncolored areas. These bright areas appear to be windows. The insect that tries to escape through these fake windows gets a rude surprise and may fall to the bottom.

A South American variety of pitcher plant traps prey in yet another way. Instead of a hood, it has a tiny platform at the opening of the pitcher. There is room on the platform for only one feeder. If two insects battle for a spot on the nectar-laden platform, one will likely fall off into the pitcher.

Some pitcher plants deaden their victim's senses with poisons. *Sarracenia flava* for example, produces a substance that acts as a narcotic. As the insect laps up the nectar it becomes less wary and less steady on its feet.

Whether it is drugged or not, once an insect starts walking among the hairs, its fate is sealed. All the hairs point downward into the pitcher. While the insect can move around the hairs as it walks into the pitcher, it finds its way blocked by these hairs when it tries to turn around.

Just past the hairs, the footing turns slippery again. This portion of the pitcher plant is smooth and waxy. Now the prey is trapped. The path back to the opening is blocked by hairs; the path ahead is impossibly slick. The creatures slip and fall into the pool of liquid at the bottom.

Here the pitcher plant has one more way to prevent escape. Some pitchers contain toxins that stun the prey. Others have a wetting agent that soaks the wings of flying insects so they cannot fly out. The wetting agent also breaks the surface tension—the force that binds water molecules together and makes it possible for many insects to crawl on the surface of water. With the surface tension destroyed, the insects drown.

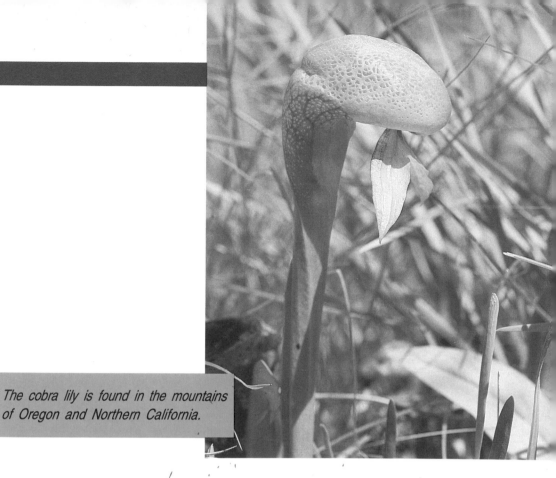

The cobra lily is found in the mountains of Oregon and Northern California.

Meanwhile enzymes trickle down the inside walls of the pitcher and collect in the bottom. Gradually, the plant digests the nutrients of the victim and absorbs them through special glands. After a time, the pool at the bottom may become filled with corpses of the plant's victims.

Pitcher plants most commonly eat ants, flies, and beetles. They will also capture and devour crickets, wasps, spiders, and even small toads.[1]

Cobra Lily

Perhaps the only carnivorous plant that truly looks deadly is a type of pitcher plant called *Darlingtonia*, the cobra lily. This plant grows in mountainous bogs in western Oregon and northern California.

Meat-Eating Plants

The cobra lily gets its name from a section of leaf, near the opening of the pitcher, that looks like the fangs or the forked tongue of a snake. With its straight stalk and rounded, spotted hood, it looks like a cobra poised to strike.

The fanglike part of the cobra lily serves as a deck to make landing even more convenient for flying insects. It is laced with nectar and hairs that lead the prey into the pitcher opening.

Nepenthes

The *Nepenthes*, found in tropical regions of Asia such as Borneo and the Philippine Islands, are similar to *Sarracenia* pitchers. These plants have long leaves that taper to a point and then form pitchers. They grow like vines, creeping along the soil and up tree trunks. Stems of *Nepenthes* may grow longer than sixty-six feet (about twenty meters).[2] The plant bears two kinds of pitchers: smaller, trumpet-shaped ones in the upper part of the plant and large, wider vases on the lower end.

Small creatures feed on nectar near the opening of the pitcher. Their feet become coated with a loose wax that causes them to slide on the slippery surface and fall into the pitcher. There they are digested in a mixture of rainwater and enzymes.

Giant Carnivorous Plants

Of all carnivorous plants, two species of *Nepenthes* come closest to the human-eating monsters of science fiction. The *Nepenthes rajah*, or King Monkey Cup, has gourdlike pitchers that may be 14 inches (35 centimeters) long and 6 inches (15 centimeters) in diameter. The pitchers of the *Nepenthes merrilliana*, found in the Philippines, may grow as large as 10 inches (25 centimeters) in diameter.[3]

These giant *Nepenthes* usually dine on cockroaches, centipedes,

Insects were the last catch of this Giant Nepenthes.

and scorpions as well as smaller insects, but they are large enough to kill bigger creatures that occasionally topple into the pitcher. Field mice, rats, small birds, and monkeylike animals called lemurs have been found dead in the bottoms of *Nepenthes*.

The Fork Traps

Genlisea is a carnivorous plant that lays a unique kind of one-way trap. This small tropical plant is found in waterlogged soil in South America, Africa, and the West Indies. The *Genlisea* sends spiraled, two-pronged forks into the ground. The forks are from one to six inches (2.5 to 15 centimeters) long.[4] A slit runs from the base of the fork down each tine. Tiny creatures can enter the slit at any point along the fork. Once they do, they are unlikely to escape. Rings of hair force the creatures in only one direction—toward a digestive chamber.

Trapped! A tiny fly meets its doom in this Venus's-flytrap.

4

TRIGGER TRAPS

Plants that use trigger traps to capture prey are perhaps the most fascinating of the carnivorous plants. Unlike the flypapers and pitchers, which lure prey to a lethal spot and digest them, trigger traps strike suddenly. Like the fierce predators of the animal world, they have something that works like a mouth to snap shut on their prey.

Venus's-flytrap

A trigger trap called *Dionaea,* or Venus's-flytrap, is found only along the coastal plains of North and South Carolina. It was unknown to most of the world until two hundred years ago. Today, because of its relatively large size and fascinating explosive action, it is probably the most famous of all carnivorous plants.

Meat-Eating Plants

This white-flowered plant usually contains a half dozen traps that may be as large as three inches (about eight centimeters) across.[1] The traps are leaves, divided into two lobes that look like a partially open clamshell. Spines line the edges of these lobes. Three trigger hairs are arranged in a triangular pattern inside the trap.

The inside of the trap is bright red. Along with the usual sugary nectar, the color helps to lure an insect close to the trigger hairs. As the insect feeds on the nectar, it brushes a trigger hair. This sends an electronic message to the rest of the leaf: Prepare for action!

The insect is now one touch away from doom. A few seconds later it bumps another trigger hair. Instantly water rushes out of the inner cells of the leaf. This causes the two lobes to snap together in a fraction of a second.

This quick action is hard on the plant. A trap can spring only three or four times before it turns black and falls off, so a Venus's-flytrap cannot afford to waste the effort. It has two ways of making sure that whatever triggers the trap is really worth eating. First, the nectar is placed far enough from the trigger hairs so that a small feeding insect will not reach them. Second, the trap will not shut unless two different hairs are touched or one hair is touched twice. This prevents the trap from closing on a piece of debris that might get blown into it.

The plant does not clamp completely shut at first. It closes just far enough for the spines to overlap, like bars on a jail cell. Again, the plant does this so as not to waste effort on small prey. The spines hold larger insects in, while smaller insects can scoot out between them. If no insect remains in the trap, it reopens within twenty-four hours.

If a suitable prey remains, the trap closes tightly. The two lobes may squeeze together so hard that the outline of the prey can be seen through the leaf. This action crushes soft-bodied insects and seals the trap so that it turns into a digestive vat. The plant releases fluids that drown the prey so that the plant can digest the nutrients. It absorbs the nutrients, using a process that may take several days. Then it reopens, exposing the undigested remains, which fall off or blow away. The Venus's-flytrap is then ready for another victim.

Actually, the Venus's-flytrap would more properly be called a Venus's ant trap, since large ants are its primary food, but it eats whatever it catches, as long as the prey is the right size. This includes flies, spiders, snails, slugs, and tiny frogs. Venus's-flytraps have even been known to eat small shrimp when the ocean floods into their domain.

Bladderworts

The plants that are most deadly to tiny aquatic creatures are the *Utricularia*, or bladderworts. They use what some botanists call "the most intricate mechanism in the plant kingdom" to snatch unsuspecting prey out of the water faster than the eye can see.[2]

The nearly three hundred species of bladderworts are the most widespread of all plant carnivores, thriving from the arctic to the tropics. They are rootless plants that float free in shallow lakes, ponds, and quiet streams, or anchor themselves loosely in water-soaked ground.

The more common aquatic forms drift along the water,

sending beautiful yellow or purple flowers above the surface. The business end of the plant lies below the surface. The bladderwort sends out a network of hairlike stems up to ten feet (three meters) in length. These stems are loaded with tiny balloonlike structures called bladders from which the plants get their name.

These bladders rarely grow as large as a quarter of an inch long—some may be no more than a hundredth of an inch. At one end of each bladder, there is a trapdoor that swings inward. Most of the time this door is sealed shut by a sticky substance.

The bladderwort sets the trap by pumping some of the water out of its bladder. This creates a partial vacuum inside the bladder. You can get the same effect by squeezing the rubber tip of an eyedropper. As soon as you release the tip, it sucks in liquid. The bladderwort's door, however, blocks water from coming into the bladder. The pressure remains, so the bladder is ready to suck in water as soon as the door opens.

Along comes a tiny water creature, so small that you would need a magnifying glass to see it. The creature begins to feed on what appear to be strands of algae. In fact, these strands are trigger hairs that surround the door opening. When the creature touches one of these

Close examination reveals tiny creatures trapped in the death chambers of this bladderwort.

hairs, the trap springs with lightning speed.

The door flies open. The pressure created within the bladder causes water to be sucked in with such force that the entire plant jerks. The water sweeps the prey in with it. As soon as the water fills the bladder, the door closes. The entire process may take as little as one five-hundredth of a second. No creature on earth is fast enough to escape a trap that springs that quickly![3]

Bladderworts living in wet soil catch microscopic worms and insects that swim in the water below the soil. Aquatic plants usually gulp only tiny invertebrates (animals without back-bones) such as water mites and mosquito larvae.

Water mites are just one of many tiny creatures snared by bladderworts.

Because their openings are so small, it would be difficult to notice bladderwort kills even when their traps are snapping left and right. Occasionally, however, the force of the trap opening snares something larger, such as a newborn fish or a tadpole. Sometimes these unfortunate creatures are found with their heads stuck in bladderwort traps. A bladderwort can ingest one of these creatures by resetting the trap with the victim's head stuck inside, and respringing the trap to suck in more. The traps can be reset within fifteen to thirty minutes.[4]

The bright yellow flower of a bladderwort offers no hint of the life and death struggle going on beneath the surface.

5

ENDLESS QUEST FOR SURVIVAL

Where did these meat-eating plants come from, and why do they attack animals? That remains a mystery. Botanists are certain that the answer to this mystery has to do with the quest for survival.

Environment   An important clue to the puzzle is the fact that most carnivorous plants live in similar types of environments. In fact, many species often live side by side. They thrive in wet, sandy, high-acid soil. This soil is a poor source of materials such as nitrogen, phosphorus, calcium, and potassium—all of which plants need to survive.

If a plant had a way to get these elements from someplace other than the soil, it would have a great advantage over other plants in these areas. Most experts believe that carnivorous plants

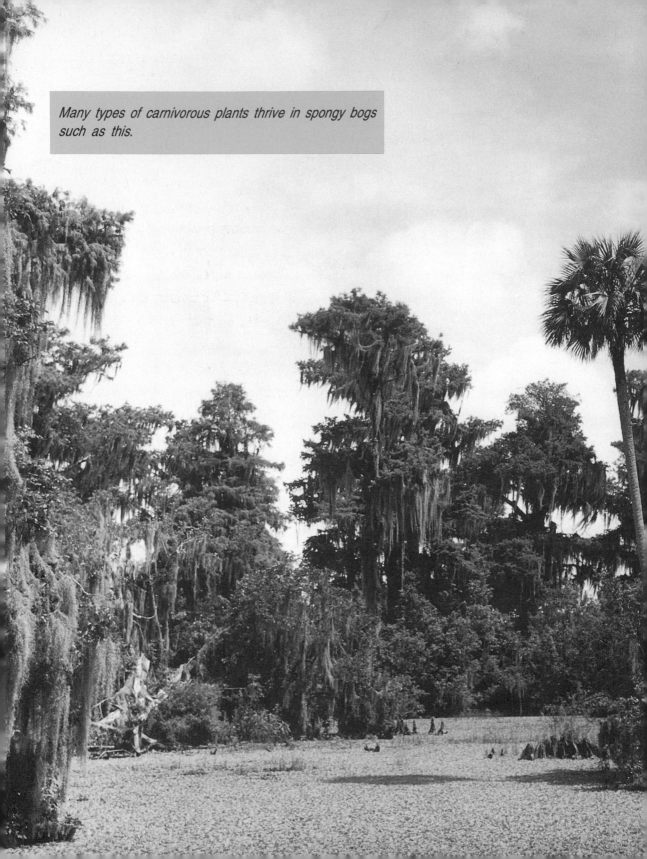

Many types of carnivorous plants thrive in spongy bogs such as this.

have done just that; they have gained an advantage in poor soil by capturing insects and other small creatures as their source of nutrients such as nitrogen and minerals.

The advantage does not appear to be large. Carnivorous plants do not need to eat creatures in order to live and grow, but these plants are not likely to be as large or as healthy as actively trapping carnivorous plants.[1] A slight addition of nutrients to the diet is particularly important when nutrients are especially scarce. The small advantage over other types of plants that carnivorous plants gain from their unusual feeding habits may be especially important during tough times.

One such time could be during a long absence of fire. While we often think of wildfires as devastating, many carnivorous plants can survive them and even thrive afterward. Most carnivorous plants grow from hardy rhizomes that are buried in the ground. These are not affected by aboveground fires. In fact, a few botanists think that carnivorous plants may need fires for their survival. Fires not only wipe out competing plants; they also release nutrients that have been soaked up by plants and return them to the soil.

Origin of Carnivorous Plants

How did carnivorous plants come up with their unusual survival strategy? How did they develop such amazing traps? Again, no one knows for sure.

One possible answer is that creature-trapping came about by accident. Many plants, not just carnivorous ones, are able to absorb nutrients through their leaves. Perhaps the original carnivorous plants had leaves that curled into shallow bowls.

Water could have collected on these leaves in shallow pools that attracted insects. Some of these visitors could have accidentally drowned. The plants then absorbed nutrients from the dead insects, which gave them a survival advantage in areas with poor soil. Over millions of years, the plants could have developed leaves that were more and more helpful at capturing small creatures.[2]

Giant People-Eating Plants

The slim survival margin that carnivorous plants gain from their activities helps answer questions about the size of these plants. People have long been fascinated with the idea of huge meat-eating plants capable of swallowing human beings. Could such creatures have existed, just as incredibly huge dinosaurs once roamed the earth?

No; nor would they ever be likely to exist. Meat eating provides a small advantage in gaining nutrients. The slight advantage is worth the energy the plant has to expend to capture and digest very small creatures. A plant would need to use a huge amount of energy to capture and digest large animals. Bladderworts have great difficulty digesting the larger organisms that they catch, and they may even die in the attempt. Venus's-flytraps turn black and die if they happen to catch a prey that is larger than what they normally can handle.

The fact that they have gained a competitive advantage does not mean that it is always easy for carnivorous plants to catch prey. Just as these plants have adapted ways to compete more efficiently, other creatures have adapted ways to beat the carnivores' tricks. A wingless insect called a caspid, for example, has developed an antidote to the sticky glue of flypaper traps. It fearlessly walks up and down leaves that mean instant death to most other insects.

A captured insect floats inside a pitcher plant.

The flower of a pitcher plant rises like a beacon over the pitchers.

Hooded pitcher plants offer shade, warmth, humidity, shelter from rain, and a ready supply of food for any creature that can avoid their deadly traps. Many insects have accepted the challenge of living dangerously. At least sixteen species of insects are found nowhere else but in pitcher plants![3] Mosquito larvae and fly maggots wriggle among the blackened carcasses in the pitcher's pool. Coated with a special substance that protects them from the plant's digestive enzymes, they feed on the rotting and half-digested remains of trapped prey.

One species of moth spins a net across the opening of the pitcher plant to form a roofed home. Protected from rain and other insects, these moths chew on the walls of the pitcher. They have no trouble crawling up and down the walls that are so deadly to most other insects. Their special claws allow them to cling to the downward-pointing hairs. They walk down the plant backward so they don't have to try to turn themselves around when they are wedged in by the hairs.

One kind of spider avoids the slippery walls of the pitcher altogether by spinning a silken lifeline on which it drops down to the bottom of the pitcher to collect meals captured by the plant. Some birds have taken advantage of the pitchers' skill at capturing food. They slit plant walls with their beaks and devour the juicy corpses they find.

The most deadly enemies of carnivorous plants are humans. People do not see much value in the boggy areas in which carnivorous plants thrive. Because of this, the natural homes of the carnivorous plants are dwindling quickly. Every year, millions of acres of these wetlands are drained, plowed under, turned into pasture or farm ponds, covered by housing or industrial developments, or paved over.

Carnivorous plants have also suffered from their own beauty. Their bright flowers and the striking network of green, purple, red, and pink veins in their leaves has made them an attractive part of floral arrangements. Millions of plants are picked for bouquets every year. Until recent laws imposed stiff penalties on harvesting Venus's-flytraps, people picked these plants just for the novelty of having them.

Care must be taken to ensure that these species survive. Otherwise the world could lose forever a fascinating group of plants—the curious little monster plants that have turned the tables on the animal world.

Chapter 1

1. Randall Schwartz, *Carnivorous Plants* (New York: Praeger, 1974), p. 118.

2. Ibid., pp. 122–123.

3. James Pietropaola, *Carnivorous Plants of the World* (Portland, Ore.: Timber Press, 1986), p. 15.

4. Michael Lipski, "Forget Hollywood: These Bloodthirsty Beauties Are for Real," *Smithsonian* (December 1992), p. 52.

Chapter 2

1. James Pietropaola, *Carnivorous Plants of the World* (Portland, Ore.: Timber Press, 1986), p. 75.

2. Ibid., p. 76.

3. Randall Schwartz, *Carnivorous Plants* (New York: Praeger, 1974), p. 24.

4. Nancy J. Nielson, *Carnivorous Plants* (New York: Facts on File, 1992), p. 33.

5. Schwartz, p. 50.

Chapter 3

Notes by Chapter

1. James Pietropaola, *Carnivorous Plants of the World* (Portland, Ore.: Timber Press, 1986), p. 15.

2. Ibid., p. 40.

3. Ibid, p. 43.

4. Adrian Slack, *Carnivorous Plants* (Cambridge, Mass.: MIT Press, 1979), p. 116.

Chapter 4

1. "Adios," *New Yorker* (July 13, 1992), p. 26.

2. John E. Mathisen, "Plants That Eat Flies," *Minnesota Volunteer* (May–June 1980), p. 42.

3. Ibid.

4. Ibid.

Chapter 5

1. Adrian Slack, *Carnivorous Plants* (Cambridge, Mass.: MIT Press, 1979), pp. 9–10.

2. Nancy J. Nielson, *Carnivorous Plants* (New York: Facts on File, 1992), p. 25.

3. Michael Lipski, "Forget Hollywood: These Bloodthirsty Beauties Are for Real," *Smithsonian* (December 1992), p. 52.

Glossary

bladder—A flexible sac that stores liquid in a plant or animal.

bog—Soggy, waterlogged ground that is high in acid and low in nutrients.

botanist—A scientist who studies plants.

carnivorous—Meat-eating.

caspid—A type of wingless fly.

enzymes—Proteins that perform or speed up chemical reactions.

invertebrates—Animals without backbones.

lemur—A small, large-eyed, tree-climbing mammal, similar in appearance to a monkey.

lobe—A rounded division or section of a larger plant or body part.

mucilage—A sticky, gummy liquid produced by plants.

nectar—A sweet liquid produced by plants.

rhizome—An underground or underwater plant stem from which the roots and shoots of certain plants arise.

rosette—A circular pattern of leaves arising from a central spot.

rotatoria—Microscopic, three-sectioned roundworms.

surface tension—The binding force between individual water molecules that holds water together at its surface.

tentacle—A sensitive hair or stalk.

toxin—A poisonous substance.

KINGDOM PLANTAE

Division Magnoliophyta (*Flowering Plants*)
Class Magniolopsida (*Dicotyledons*)

Order Nepenthales
Family Droseraceae (Sundews, flytraps)
Common Sundew (*Drosera roundifolia*)
Venus's-flytrap (*Dionaea muscipula*)

Family Nepenthaceae
King Monkey Cup (*Nepenthes rajah*)
Giant Nepenthes (*Nepenthes merrilliana*)

Classification

Order Scrophulariales
Family Lentibulariaceae
Butterwort (*Pinguicula vulgaris*)
Bladderwort (*Utricularia olivacea*)
Fork traps (*Genlisea*)

Order Sarraceniales
Family Sarraceniaceae
Common pitcher plant (*Sarracenia purpurea*)
Yellow pitcher plant (*Sarracenia flava*)
Cobra Lily (*Darlingtonia californica*)

Order Sacifragales
Family Byblidaceae
Flypaper trap (*Byblis gigantea*)

Class Liliopsida (Monocotyledon)
Family Gramineae
Killer Grass (*Molinia caerulea*)

KINGDOM FUNGI
Arthrobotrys obligiospora
Zoophagus insidians

"Adios," *New Yorker* (July 13, 1992), p. 25.

Folkerts, George. "The Gulf Coast Pitcher Plant Bogs." *American Scientist* (May–June 1982), pp. 260–267.

Lipski, Michael. "Forget Hollywood: These Bloodthirsty Beauties Are for Real." *Smithsonian* (December 1992), pp. 49–59.

Mathison, John E. "Plants That Eat Flies." *Minnesota Volunteer* (May–June 1980), p. 42.

Nielsen, Nancy J. *Carnivorous Plants*. New York: Facts on File, 1992.

Further Reading

Pietropaola, James. *Carnivorous Plants of the World*. Portland, Ore.: Timber Press, 1986.

Schwartz, Randall. *Carnivorous Plants*. New York: Praeger, 1974.

Slack, Adrian. *Carnivorous Plants*. Cambridge, Mass.: MIT Press, 1979.

———. *Insect-Eating Plants and How to Grow Them*. Seattle: University of Washington Press, 1988.

Stone, Judith. "Little Bog Man." *Discover* (February 1990), pp. 30–36.

Wexler, Jerome. *Secrets of the Venus's Fly Trap*. Nashville, Tenn.: Thomas Nelson, 1981.

———. *Sundew Stranglers: Plants that Eat Insects*. New York: Dutton Children's Books, 1994.

Index

A

Africa, 27
Alabama, 21
ants, 4, 9, 25, 28, 31
Arthrobotrys obligiospora, 9
Asia, 26
Australia, 15, 18

B

Bartram, William, 8
beetles, 25
birds, 9, 41
bladderwort (*Utricularia*), 8,
    31–34. 38
    location, 31
    flowers, 31, 34
    trapping, 31–33
bogs, 9, 22, 25, 36
Borneo, 26
Brazil, 5
butterflies, 11, 16
butterwort (*Pinguicula*), 12–14, 15
    location, 13
    trapping, 15
Byblis, 18

C

cactus, 7
California, 25
Capsella bursa-pastoris, 9
carnivorous plants
    advantages, 37
    discovery, 7, 8
    habitat for other creatures, 41
    origin, 37, 38
    size limitations, 38
    survival, 42
caspid, 38
centipedes, 26

cobra lily (*Darlingtonia*), 25, 26
cockroaches, 26
crickets, 25

D

Darlingtonia (*See* cobra lily)
Darwin, Charles, 8
Death Flower, 5
Dionaea (*See* Venus's-flytrap)
dragonflies, 17
Drosera (*See* sundew)
Drosera rotundifolia, 14

E

eelworms, 9

F

fish, 8, 9, 33
flies, 4, 9, 25, 31
flypaper traps, 13–19
frogs, 9, 18, 31

G

Genlisea, 27
gnats, 15
grasshoppers, 9

K

Killer fungi, 9, 10
Killer grasses, 9
Killer seeds, 9
King Monkey Cup (*Nepenthes
    rajah*), 26

L

lemurs, 9
Little Shop of Horrors, 6
lizards, 18

M

Madagascar, 5
mice, 9
Minnesota, 21

Molineia caerulea, 9
monkeys, 5
mosquito larvae, 9, 11, 33, 41
moths, 41

N
Nepenthes, 26–27
Nepenthes merrilliana, 26
Nepenthes rajah, (*See* King Monkey
    Cup)
North Carolina, 29

O
Oregon, 25

P
Philippine Islands, 26
Pinguicula (*See* butterwort)
Pinguicula vulgaria, 12
pitcher plants (*Sarracenia*), 20–24,
    26, 39–41
   flowers, 21, 40
   location, 22
   trapping, 21–24
pitfall traps, 20–27
plant defenses, 6, 7

R
rats, 9
rotatoria, 9

S
Sarracenia (*See* pitcher plants)
Sarracenia flava, 24
Sarracenia Purpurea, 20
scorpions, 9, 27

shrimp, 31
slugs, 9, 31
snails, 9, 31
snakes, 9
South America, 24, 27
South Carolina, 29
spiders, 9, 25, 31, 41
sundew (*Drosera*), 11, 14, 17, 18,
    19
   location, 15
   trapping, 16, 17, 18

T
tadpoles, 9, 33
toads, 25
Treat, Mary, 8
trigger traps, 29–34

U
United States, 9
Utricularia (*See* bladderwort)

V
Venus's-flytrap (*Dionaea*), 4, 7,
    28–31, 38, 42
   flower, 30
   location, 29
   trapping, 30–31

W
wasps, 9, 25
water mites, 33

Z
Zoophagus insidians, 9